The Leadership Secret of Gregory Goose

"First day ... new job ... now what?"

Gregory's transformational journey started
on the day he was promoted to lead goose.

By Judith E. Glaser

Benchmark
COMMUNICATIONS, INC.

Written by
Judith E. Glaser
CEO
Benchmark Communications, Inc.

Illustrated by
Seth Kendall

Designed by
Bobbi Benson
Green Grass Creative
Boulder, Colorado

Benchmark
COMMUNICATIONS, INC.

116 Central Park South, Suite 9D
New York, NY 10019
Tel: 212.307.4386
Fax: 212.307.0699

5 Shorehaven Road
Norwalk, CT 06855
Tel: 203.838.6982
Fax: 203.838.7166

E-Mail: jeglaser@creatingwe.com

Inspiration for Gregory Goose
Author's Personal Story

At 9:30 AM on September 11th, 2001, at the same time the World Trade Center was being attacked and destroyed and people were dying, my doctor told me that I had breast cancer. I finally reached my husband, who said, "I love you. Come home." I was at New York-Presbyterian Hospital, completely across town from where we lived. I could not find a cab, everyone was heading North away from the disaster. I was walking South back to my apartment.

As I walked home from the doctor's office in a state of numbness, I saw strangers covered with dust, hugging each other and talking about the enormous tragedy. As the world became connected around this global tragedy, my life was now on a track I have never anticipated. My husband and I were trapped in NY for a week; we couldn't even go to our home in Connecticut, since the city was shut down: no one in – no one out. The smoke and the dust covered the city.

After two operations, my highly virulent cancer lump was removed. A third operation by a plastic surgeon made me look normal again. But I was not. A bone marrow analysis showed the presence of cancer like cells, and I was scheduled for the strongest chemo to be followed by radiation.

Chemo made my hair fall out quickly, but I refused to remove the few strands that remained. They were the tough guys and I wanted to be tough. But that wasn't so easy to do. I got 'chemo-brain.' Not a lot had been written about chemo-brain in 2001, and it took me by surprise. Chemo messes with your brain, your body, your energy and your soul. I was unable to hold my thoughts in place, and my writing skills diminished to naught.

Before cancer I had started writing my first book – *Creating We: Change I-Thinking to We-Thinking & Build a Healthy Thriving Organization* however my writing came to a dead stop. I could not think. Chemo had taken its toll on my spirits and my mind. I was fearful that it had also destroyed my passion to write.

Chemo is very weird. After a two hour or more Chemo session, where you sit in a room with others with cancer, and watch this red poison go into your vein as well as coursing into everyone else's veins, you leave and you feel great. You say to yourself,

■ 3 ■

"I can handle this." But the second day, you hit the wall. You cannot move. You go from living to being a zombie, just like that. I later found that along with the chemo you are given a mood elevating drug; it is when that disappears from your brain that you crash.

One morning, after my second chemo treatment (which was delayed because the first chemo treatment had lowered my immune system activity too much and I needed a booster to pump it up), while taking a shower and praising the few strands of hair that toughed it out, a goose, of all things, appeared in my mind. By the time my shower was finished the story of Gregory had flooded out of my mind – and the *Leadership Secret of Gregory Goose* was born. I found a graphic artist – Peter Cutler – who helped me tell the story of Gregory visually. By the time my chemo treatments were completed, the first version of Gregory was also complete.

A few years ago, a colleague, Joel Marks, suggested I turn Gregory into an animated film – which I did with the help of another talented animator – Seth Kendall. And this year, with the help of Bobbi Benson my book designer – Gregory came to life in the pages of this book.

Gregory is a timeless story about leadership – true leadership. You will discover that turning to others in times of our greatest challenges, is the most transformational and powerful step a leader can take. You will learn, as Gregory learned, that leadership is not about having power-over others, it's about having power-with others. Gregory brings to life the most important leadership lessons about how to lead, and how not to lead – lessons that every leader faces every day.

Gregory will introduce you to new words; new concepts, new ideas and practices that will help you grow your leadership and trigger the leadership instincts in others.

It is now 10 years ago that the Gregory stories were born and I am cancer free. My husband says that all it took to get me back to my old self was three operations, a month of radiation and four wigs (I even had one styled by my hair dresser).

It is nice to be back.

Enjoy the journey!

The Leadership Secret of Gregory Goose

I hope this little book inspires and sparks big ideas about transformational leadership within this new millennia of rapid change and revolutionary challenges ... in the ways we view and conduct our business ... in the ways we seek and discover fulfillment ... in the ways we break down the walls to release the positive energy, the unbridled impetus – to effect positive change! This parable is based on the true story of the Canadian geese.

The True Story of
Canadian Geese

*A*s Canada Geese migrate, they fly in "V" formation. This is because the beating of their wings creates up drafts of air that support the geese. Scientists estimate that geese flying in these formations can cover 71% greater distances than a goose flying alone.

However, the lead goose is not supported by up drafts, and quickly becomes tired. To address this, the geese are constantly changing roles, with leaders dropping back into the ranks, while another moves into the leadership position. In fact, if you watch a flock of geese flying, it is constantly combining and re-combining into fluidly formed groups and sub-groups.

Moreover, the geese flying in the rear positions know the challenges of leadership because they have all had the chance to exercise its responsibilities. They are constantly "honking" to express their support and encouragement to the lead goose.

Power
Ultimate

As winter turns the air cold, geese prepare to migrate south to find another home. They survive by migrating to new territory, and this year, the flight was treacherous. The icy rains and blinding snow caused many geese to tire more quickly. Gregory took the lead on this dangerous flight, and pulled them through by drawing on an inner strength and courage to hold the line – a strength he did not even know he had. It was a challenging flight he would never forget ... most of all because Gregory was learning wisdom that changed his life forever ...

"First day, new job, now what?"
Gregory wondered ...

*G*regory's real transformational journey started the day he was promoted to lead goose.

Most humans don't know that geese get promoted. After all, geese don't move to a bigger office, the sign on the door doesn't change ... and there are no big paychecks .... Becoming the lead goose happens over time through careful observation of other lead geese. Gregory had studied all his life, and knew the power rules instinctively well

. . . or so he thought.

Rule 1

Power

Power comes from how strongly you flap your wings…

Gregory had become quite good at reading the subtle power signs. For one, there was a special way that geese flapped their wings. Powerful flaps tells other geese you are in control, and Gregory had studied power flapping all of his life, preparing for the time he would be the most powerful goose in the pond. By watching the older geese, Gregory noticed that powerful flaps pushed the other geese away, giving the lead goose a larger space to feed in. Gregory studied power-flapping, preparing for the time when he would be the most powerful goose in the pond. Flapping strongly was power

. . . or so he thought.

Rule 2

Power

Power comes from how loudly you honk

In the beginning, Gregory thought all honks were alike. He soon realized that the lead goose seemed to have a different honk. The more powerful geese honked louder than all the rest. The honks rose above the noises from the pond, and created echoes over the horizon, letting the other geese know WHO had the power. Gregory was learning by watching, listening and imitating. He would seek out less powerful geese and honk them away, testing his new found powers. Honking loudly was power

. . . or so he thought.

Power

Rule 3

Power comes from how much you honk

It was more than just loud honking that caught his attention. The more powerful geese also honked more often, causing the other geese to become silent. Sometimes for a game, Gregory would count the times the lead geese honked, and he realized a pattern he could not believe. The lead geese honked five times more than the less powerful geese. Gregory started to practice power-honking every day. At first he found he had to push hard to get his honks in when there were so many other geese around. Soon it became a game to him and he honked, and honked his way around the pond and rushes. Gregory started to practice power-honking every day, and as he did, he discovered he was moving up the pecking order

. . . or so he thought.

Rule 4

Power

Power comes from how well you Strut

During the day, many geese would meet on the pond's island. The island was very large and had three resting spots that attracted the geese from the surrounding areas. At times during the day, there were as many as 200 geese visiting the island, which Gregory named The Rushes.

Every day he observed the geese visit from distant places. Over time he recognized the patterns that at first were not visible to him as he was just a beginner. Gregory noticed the powerful geese had a way of lifting their "legs" above the rushes and the rocks when they strutted – to Gregory, they appeared fearless as they navigated over the most dangerous terrain. He was in awe, and knew he wanted to strut like that some day ... Strutting was real power

. . . or so he thought.

Power

Power comes from how fast and strong you are

$\mathcal{E}$veryday at the pond the geese had races. They lined up in a row, and at the same moment started to furiously flap their wings, propelling them forward across the very top of the pond. Gregory practiced and practiced, building his strength and his stamina, until he could win every time. Powerful geese seemed to love to win, and when they did, they would push out their chest and flap their wings wildly. Gregory was building a repertoire of power skills that — in combination — were giving him the edge he had always dreamed of

. . . or so he thought.

Power

Rule 6

Power comes from your ability to peck

Gregory's next challenge was to learn how to peck. This was his biggest fear. He saw many geese loose their beautiful feathers in pecking fights, and he was not sure he could survive the pain and humiliation were he to be the looser. He noticed that the best pecks did not dismantle feathers as much as scare others geese to submission. Gregory realized it took a lot of courage to be a master-pecker, and he was going to put his attention to understanding the best way to peck. Pecking, he knew, was the true test of a goose's leadership power — and leadership was something he was living for. Those geese who mastered this skill were the most revered

. . . or so he thought.

Power

Power comes from how well you keep other geese in line

*B*eing the best, being the lead, being out in front, that's what a goose lives for, and Gregory's time had arrived. Looking back, Gregory saw all the other geese following him and he thought, "Power comes from how well you keep the other geese in line!" However, being in the front, created new and different challenges that Gregory had not been aware of before; he was now responsible for the success of others. New feelings stirred inside of him ... they were nothing he had ever felt before.

Getting inside of leadership

One cloudy day, a group of hunters suddenly ambushed Gregory and his geese, sending shots into the air! Gregory began using his power skills, like honking, strutting and flapping — but instantly he saw they were useless ...

In a moment, he made a *Leadershift* that changed his life as a leader: he turned to the other geese and started a 'honkersation.' Together the geese strategized, and split the line into three! A new language of leadership was born — power was being shared — and Gregory trusted the geese impeccably! The hunters never caught one goose that day.

Leadershift:

Releasing the Leadership instinct in others

That night, Gregory reflected on his experiences. He realized he was learning a new lesson more important than all of the power rules.

During a moment of crisis, Gregory had turned to the other geese — trusting them to become leaders ... and they did.

Up until this time, he thought leadership was having power-over others. Now he discovered that instead of seeking power-over others, he could create power-with others ... Gregory gave this new idea a name — one that never existed for him before ... he called it co-creating.

On that day, Gregory uncovered the wisdom that "sharing power releases the leadership instincts in others." And that was also the day he decided to share his leadership secrets with everyone around the world ....

$\mathcal{G}$regory's real transformational journey started the day he was promoted to lead goose. Most geese take the lead, and live happy knowing they have reached their life's ambition. But Gregory's journey went deeper and wider – taking him to places he never expected to go.

No one taught Gregory he would face such difficult situations – and no one taught him how. No one prepared him for this very day - Gregory was on his own. Yet when the hunters came something incredible happened. Gregory instinctively turned to the other geese and they connected in a way they had never connected before. In this moment they were in sync, all searching for a new way out of the danger, which loomed below.

When the geese split the line apart into three new lines – each line was going in a different direction, creating great flapping noises in the

Co-creating Conversations®

Gregory saw the light ... and flew off to another pond to share his new wisdom with everyone, everywhere!

air. The three new lead geese began calibrating with each other — in almost silent honks — letting each other know where to go and where not to go. They were in sync yet going in different directions. Some geese dove low, others dove high. They created a new set of signals and every one was learning them in real-time — it was an exhilarating day!

On his journey, Gregory uncovered a wisdom that today has taken him around the world over and over again. Gregory learned how to have Co-creating Conversations® — distinctly different conversations that releases power in others. Rather than focusing only on protecting his power, Gregory learned how to open the space for leadership power to grow and expand in others.

In the quiet of his mind, he tried to put his insights into words so he could share them with others. Rather than focusing on growing his own positional power, and using his energy to keep other geese in line, he realized he must draw power from others. By giving the other geese "leadership challenges" bigger than what they thought they could accomplish, they stepped up and discovered their personal leadership power. By opening the space for other geese to ascend to leadership, each one discovered a power they never knew they had.

Bringing Gregory Goose to Life!
Try this . . .

Every leader faces new challenges bigger than what they faced before. We are not expected to know all the answers, to have all the solutions or to be fully responsible for making all the decisions.

Each of us has unique perspectives that can be valuable when addressing our largest challenges, and the best leaders draw out insights and perspectives from others — this is the most vital part of leadership.

Specifically, Gregory learned that it's important to turn to others in the face of big challenges, and to co-create new ways to address these challenges.

Reflect:

How would you make a Leadershift?

Take a moment and reflect on your leadership challenges at work, and think about new situations coming up where you could turn to your teams to have a vital Co-creating Conversation®. Based on what you learned in this book, how might you change your next conversations? What would you do differently?

_____

_____

_____

_____

_____

_____

_____

Think about an up and coming situation where you traditionally had the mindset of 'power over' others. Make a Leadershift and think about the situation again with a 'power with' mindset. How would you approach the situation differently?

_____

_____

_____

_____

_____

_____

Expand:

Now that you've had a chance to reflect on your own leadership you can see the positive effects that your 'power-with' mindset can have on your relationships, your teams, your conversations and your organizations' success. Let's take one more look at the distinctions and definitions of the new terms in this book to see how you can leverage these new terms back in the workplace.

· What can you do more of to expand your co-creating abilities?

_____

_____

_____

_____

_____

· What can you do more of to practice 'power-with' others?

_____

_____

_____

_____

_____

· What can you do more of to trigger the leadership instincts in others?

_____

_____

_____

_____

_____

Leverage Success:

Think about how you can sustain a productive, trusting and supportive work environment that brings out the leadership instincts in others. What can you do over the next 30-60-90 days? Take a minute and develop your game plan.

- What are the practices you can envision experimenting with in your organization to unlock the Leadership Secret of Gregory Goose?

  _____

  _____

- What can you do more of to create a more inclusive workplace?

  _____

  _____

- How can you have conversations about these ideas with others?

  _____

  _____

- Who would you involve?

  _____

  _____

- What would you do in the next 30-60-90 days?

  _____

  _____

- How will you measure success?

  _____

  _____

About Benchmark Communications, Inc.

Creating WE Culture Transformation

Imagine what would be possible if your organization could intentionally shift to a new way of communicating, a new way of innovating, and a new way of thinking that was steeped in trust, mutual accountability and support!

Our Creating WE approach to Culture Transformation is designed for executives who are trying to make the shift to a more collaborative and engaging work environment that nurtures and develops talent, attracts customers, and achieves incredible profitability and business growth. We call this *'moving from I to WE.'*

During times of change, it's easy for executives to get drawn into their own silos, working issues that they can control. However, managing the larger enterprise issues is a collaborative and co-creative experience.

Our Culture Transformation process will give leaders new perspectives, frameworks and tools for moving into enterprise thinking, by reducing competitiveness and risk, and building peer support to help execute the enterprise challenges. No work is more important for a leader than creating a culture in which all team members can fully contribute.

Before most employees will share their ideas and insights, leaders must create the environment for sharing and innovation to emerge — it doesn't happen by telling people what to do or how to do it. To build a world-class organization, employees must experience the power of what "WE" can do for everyone.

What if you could create a culture with mutual accountability? One where people acted like owners, working in concert with each other to differentiate your brand and capture the hearts, minds, and souls of your customers?

Creating WE Culture Transformation is a process that will raise the collective IQ of your organization, and will pay big dividends as your business gleans new ideas and strategies, new innovation, and improved processes for running your business and reaching customers.

Our clients invest time and resources in Culture Transformation, knowing that their success comes through their people. By investing in engaging and empowering their talent they will create a healthy, committed, and inspired workforce poised to become a world-class company with sustainability and staying power.

What We Believe:

Change is about shifting strategy — and culture drives strategy. Therefore, the biggest challenge leaders face today is how to engage the organization in working strategically toward common goals; the larger the organization, the larger the challenge.

For many people, change often triggers fear, anxiety and resistance, while for others it opens up new opportunities for growth. We work with our clients during transformational initiatives to help create a context for change. We help executives learn how to engage with their people in ways that reduce resistance and create a positive energy for change. Executives experience ways of drawing out the wisdom and talent from inside the organization, and build organizational ownership, leadership and commitment to results.

Regardless of what business challenges we're asked to work on, our powerful engagement technologies help executives successfully architect strategic change during the most challenging times, such as pre- and post- mergers and acquisition, customer-centric transformations and brand building. Every client engagement is designed to elevate the organization's ability to drive the change process from within – to raise the Cultural and Brand IQ – and to set standards of excellence that ensure a leadership position in their industry.

Our Services: Setting Benchmarks for Success

Benchmarks for Building Strong Brands:
Living the Brand and Organizational Storytelling
When a culture lives the brand, it means that employees are engaged with each other in understanding and interpreting the brand and executing it at every touch point with the customer. Often, when the brand is less differentiated, employees are working everyday without the sight to the customer and without the realization of how their enterprise uniquely delivers what it says it will. When employees learn to live the brand, they resonate a high level of valued expertise in concert with each other and provide outstanding service in a way not available anywhere else. Benchmark offers our clients processes for heightening awareness of the brand and for delivering against the brand's promise. The result is more customer loyalty, brand recognition and spirit.

Enterprise Engagement: Turning Resistance into Opportunities for Change

Clients often call us because they are undergoing strategic changes in their organization. They want help in architecting the change process so that they get the maximum support and contributions of their organization to build a strong enterprise. Some clients experience resistance, territoriality and conflicts during change. In these instances, we provide expert consulting on how to set a context for change that shifts the focus from resistance, territoriality and conflicts to strengthening the enterprise.

Benchmarks for Building Strong Leaders:

Executive Coaching

For 30 years, Benchmark has served as an Executive Coach to executives in C-level positions and those moving up into C-level positions. Our coaching process is designed to assist senior executives in handling the challenges of a rapidly changing environment. We do that by helping them recognize the impact they are having, by expanding their leadership awareness and strengthening their focus as they move into their senior roles. In all cases, executives expand their capacity to positively influence the organization to achieve success. Through our coaching process we help executives explore their leadership aspirations, focus on developmental opportunities for growth, address blind spots, and practice innovative ways to tackle their leadership challenges at work.

The First 100 Days™

The First 100 Days are the most critical in defining the executive's future success. When an executive joins a company, they face new challenges such as understanding the culture, assessing the talent, and sizing up the opportunities, so they are able to positively influence the organization to move forward toward it's goals. Are they bonding with others, taking a stand, or alienating people from supporting the mission? Benchmark works with executives in new positions to help them create a platform for leadership and organizational success. We have developed a CEO Playbook that helps an executive focus on what's important and essential for success. We have developed Leadership and CEO Playbooks that help executives starting a new position focus on what's important and essential for organizational and personal success.

Senior Leadership Alignment™

Senior executive teams in organizations are often challenged to make the toughest decisions, decide on priorities, and create alignment and direction for the organization. More often than not these senior leaders and their teams do not work in concert with each other. Benchmark Communication has evolved coaching and intervention technologies that support open, honest communication and at the same time reduce executive tensions and conflicts. These processes include a combination of one-on-one coaching coupled with team consulting and enterprise interventions to help create alignment develop trust and openness and focus attention on how to successfully achieve the larger enterprise commitments and priorities.

Benchmarks for Building Strong Cultures:

Cultural Scan - DNA Assessment

Culture drives strategy. It can either enable or disable the realization of the enterprise's goals. Benchmark Communications performs Cultural Assessments that make the dynamics that are driving a culture more visible. Through this process we help executives understand how to address internal issues that are preventing the enterprise from realizing its potential. In addition we unearth internal best practices and expand on opportunities to help differentiate the culture and brand. With this information, executives will have a new handle on how to lead more effectively, how to charter and sponsor strategic projects, and how to facilitate enterprise shifts to guide the organization toward collaboratively achieving its goals.

Strategic Initiatives, Team Challenges and Action Learning

People learn most from doing. With this spirit in mind, Benchmark Communications has developed an expertise in working with senior teams to identify Team Challenges aligned with achieving new enterprise goals. Our Team Challenge Technology builds competencies in collaboration, cross-functional project management and execution. Through Team Challenges, executive teams discover how to execute work with a profound impact on the bottom line, on customer retention and loyalty and on the organization's ability to develop new competencies that sustain growth and leadership.

Leadership Journeys and Culture Integration

We work with the leadership team to architect a process for integrating their organization (often after M & A's) around the new enterprise vision, goals, strategic initiatives, projects and people, building a line of site to their customer. Leadership Journeys are enterprise interventions (Leadership Expanding Workshops) that elevate the Cultural IQ of an organization and create a powerful common ground for uniting disparate parts of the organization. They are "defining moments" for leaders in organizations where each person both individually and collectively comes face-to-face with the challenging dynamics, the obstacles, the opportunities and the possibilities for their future and by working through them together elevate the enterprise's capacity for becoming a powerful brand. The result of this process is a realization of common goals and strategies that create a new level of enterprise and brand focus.

Contact us to find out how you can bring *Creating WE* and *The Leadership Secret of Gregory Goose* to your organization!

Benchmark Communications, Inc.
www.BenchmarkCommunicationsInc.com
www.CreatingWEInstitute.com
www.CreatingWE.com
www.JudithEGlaser.com

116 Central Park South 9-D	Norwalk, CT 06855
New York, NY 10019	Tel: 203.838.6982
Tel: 212.307.4386	Fax: 203.838.7166
Fax: 212.307.0699	

Judith E. Glaser, CEO
Benchmark Communications, Inc.

Judith E. Glaser is one of the most innovative and pioneering change agents and executive coaches in the consulting industry, and is the world's leading authority on WE-centric Leadership. She often refers to herself as an Organizational Anthropologist who works at the intersection of leadership, culture and brand. Judith is the founder of Benchmark Communications, Inc., and the Co-founder of the Creating WE Institute. Her clients include many of the top Fortune 500 companies. Through Benchmark's innovative Creating WE technologies, she helps leaders focus on competitive challenges in a world of moving targets. Her highly engaging and provocative keynotes, consulting, workshops and summits catalyze transformation at the individual, team and organizational levels — leading to higher levels of productivity, profitability and business success.

Judith is the author of 2 best selling books: *Creating WE: Change I-Thinking to We-Thinking & Build a Healthy Thriving Organization, The DNA of Leadership*, and was the Editor and Co-author of *42 Rules for Creating WE*, also a best seller. Glaser is also a widely recognized thought leader on leadership in both academic circles and the public media. Judith regularly appears on TV such as NBC Today, ABC, FOX, CNN on topics such as Bully Bosses, and is quoted in the NY Times, WSJ and Harvard Business Review, and has spoken at Universities Globally including Kellogg Graduate School of Management, Harvard Business School, and University of Stellenbosch Business School.

Books by Judith E. Glaser

Creating WE
Change I-Thinking to WE-Thinking & Build a Healthy, Thriving Organization

Creating WE rejects traditional approaches to leadership and change. This revolutionary book provides breakthrough strategies for moving from an 'I to a WE' culture by changing our mindsets and the quality of our conversations. You'll gain new insights for confronting adversaries, giving critical feedback, acting as a peer coach, identifying your "fear habit patterns" and dissolve "case building" among colleagues. *Creating WE* offers touching and profound anecdotal stories drawn from Glaser's work with large clients such as Clairol, Donna Karan International, Revlon and others. Whether your company has recently been acquired, merged, restructured, downsized, or, is in the midst of rapid growth and expansion, *Creating WE* will provide a roadmap for creating and sustaining change.
Available as a Paperback and Kindle Edition.

42 Rules | for Creating WE
Edited by Judith E. Glaser
Forward by Angela Ahrendts, CEO, Burberry Group PLC

42 Rules For Creating WE is the celebrated, collaborative effort of best selling author, Judith E. Glaser and 18 of her fellow Creating WE Institute Members & Co-founders. From cutting edge neuroscientific findings to profound insights gleaned over thousands of engagements in business consulting, branding and beyond, *'42 Rules'* delivers a wealth of innovative ways for putting 'WE-centric' thinking into practice in your organization and workplace NOW!
Available as a Paperback and Kindle Edition.

The DNA of Leadership
*Leverage Your Instincts To: **Communicate, Differentiate, Innovate***

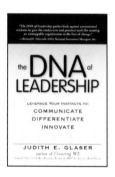

Alter a Company's DNA, and Accelerate Its Profits! Just as your DNA may determine your destiny, a company's organizational DNA may determine its destiny. The DNA of Leadership helps you understand how to shape your company's genetic code for success. Expert author Judith E. Glaser identifies the seven vital leadership practices that can reshape an organization into a WE-centric culture-a culture that enables people to effectively work together during times of organizational change. "Graft" these seven practices onto meetings, conversations, and strategic initiatives, and you can leverage talent, maximize results, and boost profits in amazing ways. Includes profiles of seven major companies, including: VeriSign, New Wave Entertainment, Dreyer's and Edy's Grand Ice Cream, and IBM.
Available as a Paperback and Kindle Edition.

Discovering the Power of WE
Why Some Leaders Succeed and Others Fail

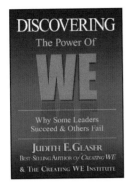

Our brains are designed to be social. Our need for belonging is more powerful than our need for safety. When we are rejected, we experience pain in the same centers in the brain and body as when we are in a car crash. Being emotionally orphaned is more painful than death. When others show us love, respect, and honor us, it triggers the same centers in the brain as when we eat chocolate, have sex, or are on drugs. Learning this will change how you lead.

Discovering the Power of WE is a book written by Judith E. Glaser in collaboration with members of The Creating WE Institute, and is filled with insights and wisdom about how our social brain works, and how to build a WE-centric workplace full of energy, innovation and engagement designed to achieve audacious personal and business results. *Discovering the Power of WE* will give you new insights and practices you can use at work immediately to shift from an "I to a WE" culture.

Discovering the Power of WE provides a step-by step guide for becoming a WE-centric leader, from understanding how to reduce the fear that triggers underperformance, to building accountability into the DNA of your culture. In this book you will learn about the power of WE-centric storytelling, how rituals trigger our bonding instincts for collaboration, and how positive emotional contagion can radically transform your workplace. You'll learn about cutting edge leadership practices, how to bring integrity and candor to work, and how to create sustainable leadership at all levels of your organization.

Discovering the Power of WE includes new insights from the world of Neuroscience of WE, and the Wisdom of Our Five Brains. Each chapter gives powerful take aways that are essential for leadership success. *Discovering the Power of WE* teaches you how to create breakthroughs that will change your leadership approach forever. You will discover your own personal power and influence for becoming a WE-centric leader, and for teaching others to become one also. The book gives you a well laid out roadmap for leadership success.
Available as a Paperback and Kindle Edition.

Multimedia | The Leadership Secret of Gregory Goose

First time leaders to C-suite executives have identified with Gregory's story – now you can learn and use Gregory's leadership secret, too!

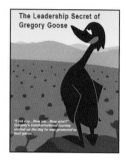

Created by Judith E. Glaser, author of *Creating We* and *The DNA of Leadership*, this in-depth workshop includes an animated video, comprehensive Facilitator's Guide and a PowerPoint Presentation. *The Leadership Secret of Gregory Goose* is a fresh way to understand how sharing power releases leadership instincts in others.

The Learning Objectives of Gregory Goose workshop are:
- Identify the difference between old leadership and new leadership (positional power vs. relational power).
- Define key terms: co-creating, power-over, power-with, inclusion, Co-creating Conversations® and leadershift.
- Examine feelings and beliefs about leadership and how to make the shift from power-over to power-with leadership.
- Create inclusive Co-creating Conversations® and practices in the workplace to strengthen relationships with direct reports, peers and colleagues and to achieve business results.
- Develop an action plan for expanding inclusive and co-creative leadership practices and conversations in the workplace.

Available as a DVD and workbook (includes Facilitators Guide & PowerPoint Presentation)

Find Judith's books on

www.BenchmarkCommunicationsInc.com, www.CreatingWE.com
and www.Amazon.com.

Made in the USA
Lexington, KY
30 April 2014